Suffolk Libraries	
30127 08676459 9	
Askews & Holts	May-2019
J513.211	£12.99

MONSTER MATHS

COUNTING

WRITTEN BY
MADELINE TYLER

ILLUSTRATED BY
AMY LI

BookLife PUBLISHING

©2019
BookLife Publishing Ltd.
King's Lynn
Norfolk PE30 4LS

ISBN: 978-1-78637-579-7

Written by:
Madeline Tyler

Edited by:
John Wood

Designed/Illustrated by:
Amy Li

All rights reserved.
Printed in Malaysia.

A catalogue record for this book is available from the British Library. All facts, statistics, web addresses and URLs in this book were verified as valid and accurate at time of writing. No responsibility for any changes to external websites or references can be accepted by either the author or publisher.

PHOTO CREDITS

All images courtesy of Shutterstock. With thanks to Getty Images, Thinkstock Photo and iStockphoto.

Cover, Page 1 & Page 2 – memphisslim, jojje, Dmitrijj Skorobogatov, Abscent. Master Images – jojje (grid), Dmitrijj Skorobogatov (illustration texture), Abscent (pattern), cluckva ()wallpaper texture, arigato, First_emotion (floors), Adelyne Tumanskaya, Bipsun, wenami (wallpaper patterns), Amy Li (all illustrations). P3 – Olga Drozdova, P4-5 – Alexander_DG, Off_abstract, P6-7 – Ambient Ideas, Dana Zurkiyeh, gresei, Ruth Black, P8-9 – Svajatoslav Andreichyn, Alias Ching, Chinnapong, P10-11 – Hajrudin Hodzic, Alexander_DG, Off_abstract, P12–13 (See master images)m P14-15 – abimages, Abstractor, Hajrudin Hodzic, gresei, Ruth Black, Kloss13, Popov Nikolay, sripfoto, P16-17 – Teerapun, Sergei Mishchenko, NataLT, I'm friday, Gita Kulinitch Studio, Feng Yu, P18-19 – A. Narloch, Christin Lola, Iliveinoctober, JennyPicsmix, leungchopan, p20-21 – Svjatoslav Andreichyn, samritk, P22-24 – see previous pages for recurring images.

This is Addy.

Addy is excited.
Today is a very special day.

Today is Addy's birthday party!

For her party, she needs one birthday cake.

There it is! ONE yummy cake.

1

TWO piñatas for the party.

1

2

3

One, two, THREE!

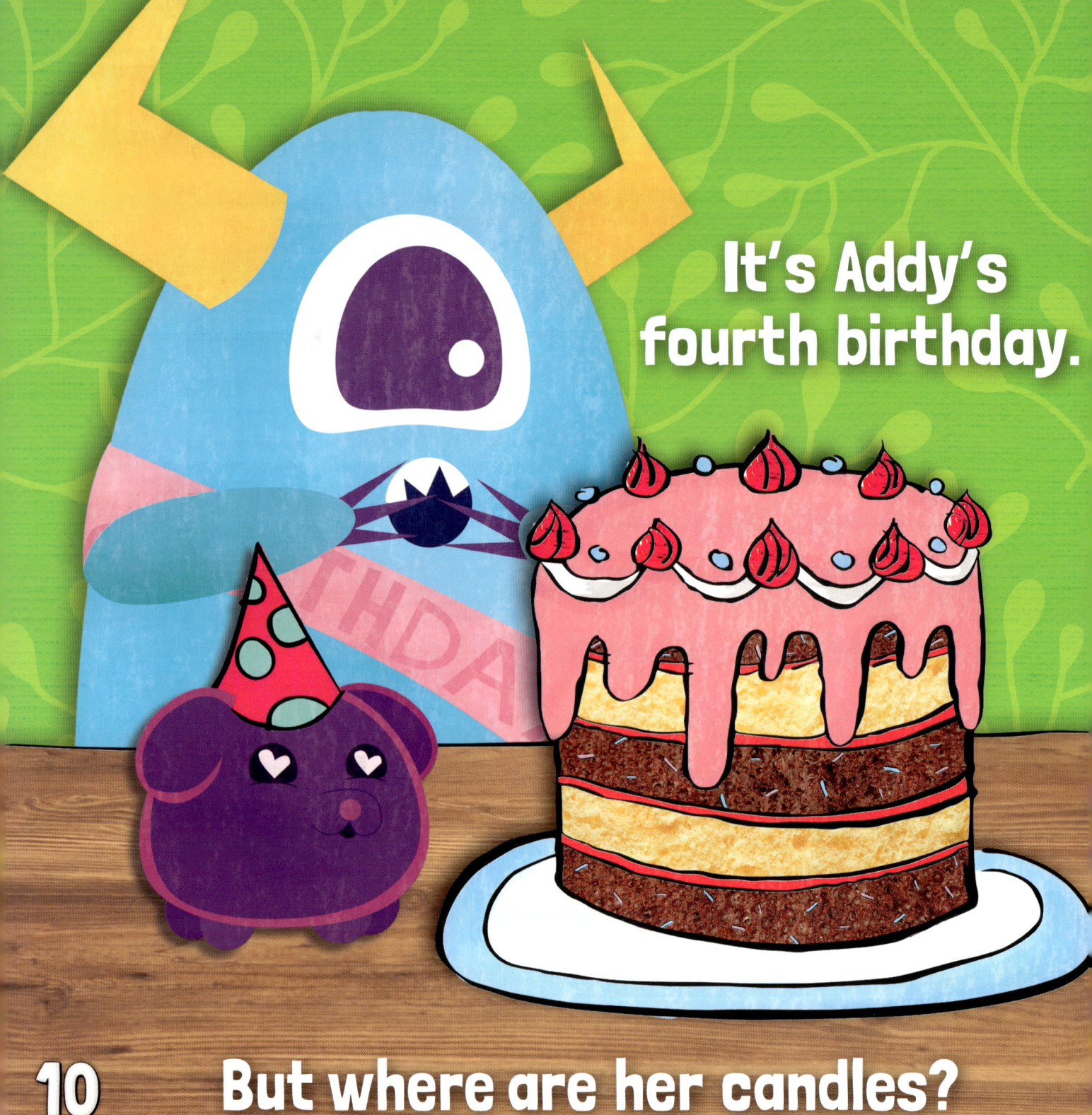

It's Addy's fourth birthday.

But where are her candles?

FOUR candles for the cake.

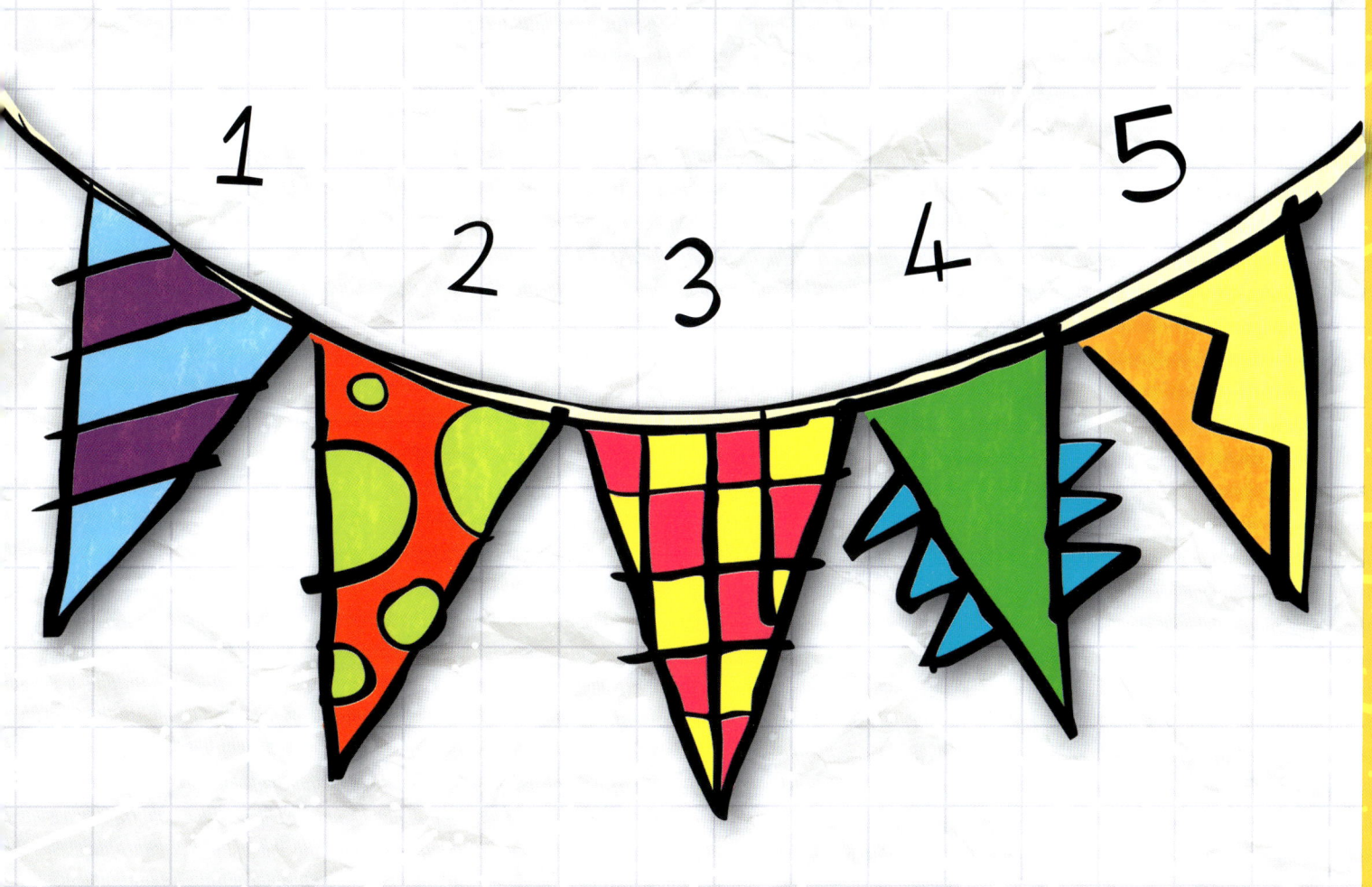

One, two, three, four, FIVE flags.

Addy is hungry. She needs six plates of party food.

SIX plates of food. Yum yum!

There they are! SEVEN tails.

It's not a party without balloons!
Can you count them?

EIGHT colourful balloons.

TEN party monsters!